Delicious Pasta Cookbook

25 Quick and Easy Pasta Recipes

Roy Holt

Text Copyright © Roy Holt

All rights reserved. No part of this guide may be reproduced in any form without permission in writing from the publisher except in the case of brief quotations embodied in critical articles or reviews.

Legal & Disclaimer

The information contained in this book and its contents is not designed to replace or take the place of any form of medical or professional advice; and is not meant to replace the need for independent medical, financial, legal or other professional advice or services, as may be required. The content and information in this book has been provided for educational and entertainment purposes only.

The content and information contained in this book has been compiled from sources deemed reliable, and it is accurate to the best of the Author's knowledge, information and belief. However, the Author cannot guarantee its accuracy and validity and cannot be held liable for any errors and/or omissions. Further, changes are periodically made to this book as and when needed. Where appropriate and/or necessary, you must consult a professional (including but not limited to your doctor, attorney, financial advisor or such other professional advisor) before using any of the suggested remedies, techniques, or information in this book.

Upon using the contents and information contained in this book, you agree to hold harmless the Author from and against any damages, costs, and expenses, including any legal fees potentially resulting from the application of any of the information provided by this book. This disclaimer applies to any loss, damages or injury caused by the use and application, whether directly or indirectly, of any advice or information presented, whether for breach of contract, tort, negligence, personal injury, criminal intent, or under any other cause of action.

You agree to accept all risks of using the information presented inside this book.

You agree that by continuing to read this book, where appropriate and/or necessary, you shall consult a professional (including but not limited to your doctor, attorney, or financial advisor or such other advisor as needed) before using any of the suggested remedies, techniques, or information in this book.

Table Of content

Introduction	6
Chapter 1: Classic Pasta dishes	8
1) Spaghetti Amatriciana	8
2) Pasta gricia	11
3) Spaghetti Carbonara	14
4) Penne with bacon and zucchini	17
5) Fettuccine with artichokes and shrimp tails	20
6) Spaghetti aglio, olio e peperoncino	23
7) Penne all'Arrabbiata	26
8) Spaghetti col rancetto	29
9) Tagliatelle con pesto di salvia	32
10) Spaghetti alla puttanesca	35
11) Spaghetti cacio e pepe	38
12) Pasta con ragù ai funghi	41
13) Spaghetti alle vongole	44
14) Spaghetti Fagioli e cozze	47
15) Pasta al verde con gamberetti	50
16) Rigatoni con carciofi, olive e capperi	53
17) Spaghetti al Tonno	56

18) Pasta al gorgonzola gratinata al forno   59

19) Pasta radicchio e zola   62

20) Tonnarelli al pesto di rucola   65

Chapter 2: Vegetarian Pasta dishes 68

1) Pasta con le melanzane   68

2) Pasta alla carrettiera   71

3) Pasta coi fagiolini   74

4) Pasta e ricotta   77

5) Pasta alla checca   80

Conclusion   83

Introduction

In this book, we present a quick overview of Italy's most popular traditional pasta dishes, homemade versions or more elaborated recipes done by chefs.

When talking about pasta, Italy is beyond compare the world's biggest producer and consumer without any doubt. Italian people are maybe the only people happy to eat pasta more than once every day.

With over 300 different dishes, from the most common ones to the regional varieties of freshly made pasta, the Italian cuisine it's considered the most refined with an endless number of possible combinations of ingredients.

Without being heavy, the Italian food can be characterized as bold and very satisfying. It is also rich in flavor, textural and uses a whole palette of ingredients. While tasting the Italian food your brain goes in a deeply emotional and satisfying state which cannot be described in words.

Pasta are considered (and cooked) as the main course and not as a basic carbohydrate to accompany meals as a side dish. They are served most likely after entrées and before meat/fish courses, which makes it a delicious example of typical Italian inventiveness.

A typical Italian meal will start with a plate of antipasti, consisting of vegetables (like mushrooms, pepperoncini, and artichoke hearts) and cured meats (like capicola and prosciutto). After that, it moves on to a small pasta dish, followed by a light protein, perhaps a leg of lamb deliciously prepared. The Italian meal gets simpler by each step, and tend to have a reverse swell.

From the initial swell to the last savored bite, every Italian dish is built upon the most basic flavorful ingredients. The traditional products are very important in the flavors of Italy cuisine, which are based on seasonality and locality.

Olive oil is one of the most important ingredients of the Italian kitchen (used for braising and frying). Beside the olive oil, the vegetables cannot miss the plate. Also, the balsamic vinegar takes a big spot in the Italian kitchen, and it's hard to find a cook without a wedge of Grana Padano or Parmigiano-Reggiano.

When you opt for making your pasta dish, you have to find the right way to bring the flavors of /Italy to your table. First, try some recipes that have only two or three ingredients and start making a quick and delicious sauce. If the palate needs to be lighter, then you should add some vegetables, like broccoli shoots.

Finally, remember that a good Italian dish starts with choosing the right ingredients. You should buy quality ingredients when you're trying to bring the Italian cuisine to your kitchen. When you finally found a dish that you love, stick with it, and practice until you can do it again! That's how Italians do.

Chapter 1: Classic Pasta dishes

1) Spaghetti Amatriciana

The Amatriciana spaghetti are a symbol of the Italian culinary tradition. The original recipe comes from Amatrice, a small town of Lazio.

Before, this recipe was a poor meal of shepherds and it contained only noodles, bacon, cheese. During the time, the recipe was included in Roman kitchen and has undergone several modifications.

Prep Time: 10 min

Cooking time: 15 min

Portions: 4 servings

Ingredients:

- 320 g Spaghetti
- 1 g Fresh chili
- 100 g Jowl
- 1 pinch of Black pepper
- 10 g Extra virgin olive oil
- 350 g Peeled tomatoes (or tomato paste)
- 75 g Romano cheese
- 50 ml White wine

Instructions:

To prepare the spaghetti Amatriciana first start cutting your chili into very thin strips. After you take the bacon, remove the tough rind and cut into thin slices and then into strips of 0.5 centimeters long. Now take a pan and pour a little oil.

In a pot, pour the bacon cut into strips: mix it using a spatula so that the cooking is uniform. The fat part of the pillow has become transparent. Nuanced now the pillow with white wine and let it evaporate, continuing to cook. Pour some red pepper.

When the wine has faded, remove from heat the bacon, drain and remove the bacon from the pans and place it in a small bowl and try to keep them warm. Meanwhile, start with the preparation of the jowl. Cut them in half and deprive them of the seeds inside.

Pour the tomatoes into the pan in which you did cook the bacon for you to absorb its sauce left in the pan for baking. Cook the tomatoes until it proves not totally dissolved. Now take a large saucepan and pour in the water. Bring it until it boils and put some salt. When the water starts to boil, bring in the spaghetti paid.

Pour the spaghetti into the pan in which you are dissolving the tomatoes and add the bacon that you kept warm. Mix well the spaghetti with the sauce and the bacon to mix the ingredients well. At this point, grated pecorino cheese on your spaghetti and ground black pepper to give to your spaghetti Amatriciana an even stronger flavor.

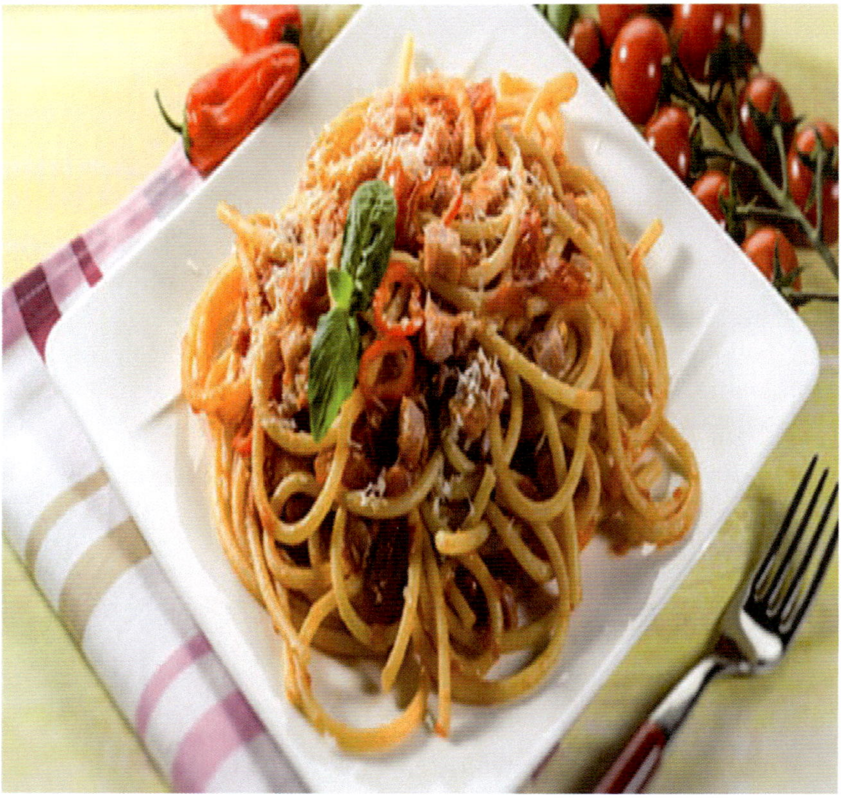

2) Pasta gricia

Pasta gricia it's considered the ancestor of pasta Amatriciana, and is one of the most famous dishes of the Lazio cuisine. The common ingredients used are: jowl, the Roman pecorino and pepper. The tomato is absent in the greasy recipe, since its origin would even prior to the importation of tomato in Europe.

It is said that to the pasta gricia was invented by the shepherds of Latium, which with few ingredients they had available to return from the pastures have created a very simple dish but equally delicious. You can choose whether dressing pasta format (long pasta, noodles are allowed, bucatini and tonnarelli, or short). In this recipe we are using the rigatoni!

Preparation: 10 min

Cooking Time : 15 min

Portions: 4 servings

Ingredients:

- Rigatoni 320 g
- Jowl 250 g
- Romano Cheese, hard 55 g
- Fine salt to taste
- Black pepper to taste

Instructions:

To prepare the dough gricia start throwing the rigatoni in plenty of lightly salted water. By the time the pasta is cooking cut the bacon into strip slices, but not too thin.

In a nonstick skillet, sauté the bacon until it becomes transparent and begins to lose its fat, forming a delicious sughino. Add a generous grinding of pepper and long with a ladle of pasta cooking water.

Drain the rigatoni and sauté with the bacon, if necessary by adding a few tablespoons of cooking water. Serve and sprinkle each dish with grated pecorino Romano. Your dough gricia is now ready to be served.

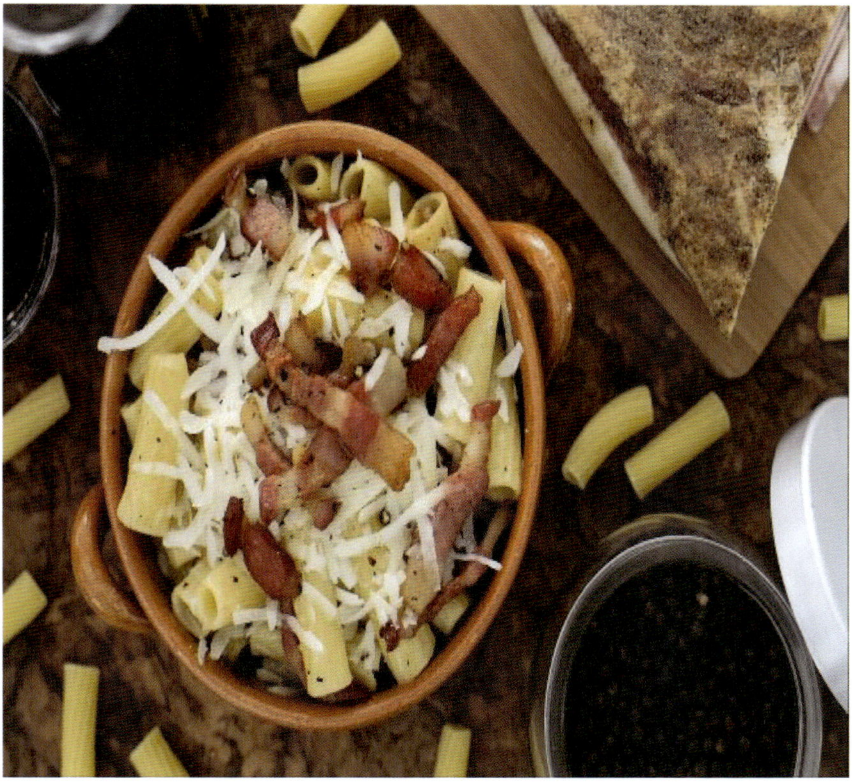

3) Spaghetti Carbonara

The origin of spaghetti carbonara is not well known. Someone says that Umbrian Carbonari first introduced this dish in the 19th century into the Roman kitchen.

It is also said that the spaghetti carbonara was invented during the WW2 when the Americans brought in large quantities of bacon and powdered eggs, which were part of military rations; by the inspiration of the Roman cooks this dish was made. It is a simple and at the same time a very tasty dish.

Preparation: 15 min

Cooking time: 10 min

Portions: 4 servings

Ingredients:

- 320 g Spaghetti
- 150 g Jowl
- 100 g Pecorino Romano
- Black pepper (optional – for taste)
- 4 yolks

Instructions:

For preparing spaghetti carbonara take a saucepan and put some water to boil. Add moderately a little of salt. Meanwhile, cut the bacon into small cubes (or strips) and put it in a frying pan.

After the fat from the bacon will become transparent and crunchy, add some oil and leave it a few minutes more.

Into a small bowl break the eggs, add the Pecorino cheese, ground pepper (according to taste) and mix everything well until you obtain a homogeneous mixture.

Add the bacon to the previously prepared sauce. You can serve the spaghetti immediately and you can add more Pecorino and/or ground black pepper.

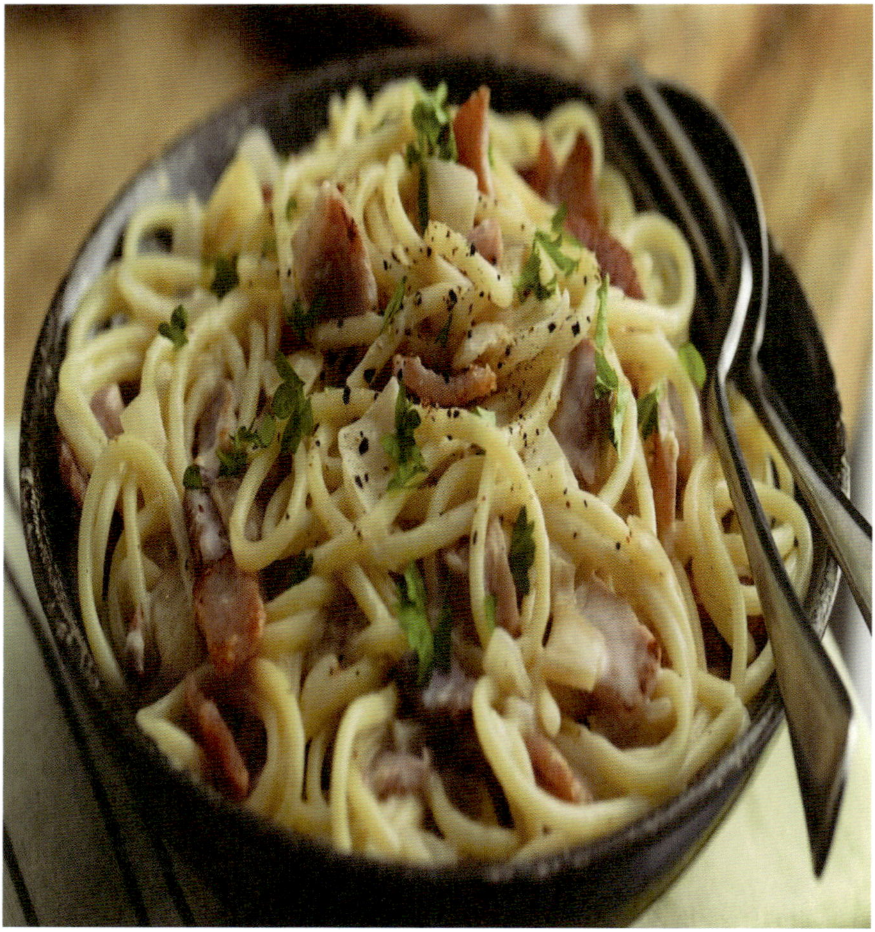

4) Penne with bacon and zucchini

This recipe you can prepare for lunch, when you don't really want to engage in more elaborate dishes. In this recipe, we chose whole-grain pasta which with its slightly toasted flavor blends perfectly with the strong taste of bacon. Everything is wrapped by the sweetness of zucchini that makes it a very balanced dish.

Preparation: 15 min

Cooking Time: 20 mins

Portions: 4 servings

Ingredients:

- Integral penne Rigate 320 g
- Zucchini 3 for a total of 360 g
- Speck in a single slice 310 g
- Shallot 60 g
- salt to taste
- Black pepper to taste
- Extra virgin olive oil 40 g
- Thyme 4 sprigs

Instructions:

After washing the zucchini cut them in half lengthwise, until you get them into 2-3 cm strips. Finally, chop the shallot and place in a saucepan along with 30 grams of oil.

Let it wither adding a ladle of hot water and add the grated zucchini, salt, pepper, still add a ladle of hot water and cook for about ten minutes, until they wilt. Meanwhile, pour 30 grams of remaining oil in a pan and add the zucchini sticks.

Add salt and pepper and cook these for 8-10 minutes. Meanwhile slice bacon of about 3 cm long strips.

Set aside 60 grams of bacon that will serve as the final seal of the dish and pour the remainder in the now cooked zucchini and cook for about 5 minutes. Meanwhile, cook the whole penne in boiling water and salt (to taste). After that, pour into the pan with the zucchini and bacon.

Stir to combine ingredients, then add the zucchini sticks, the thyme leaves. Decorate each plate with the bacon strips and serve your bacon penne and zucchini still hot!

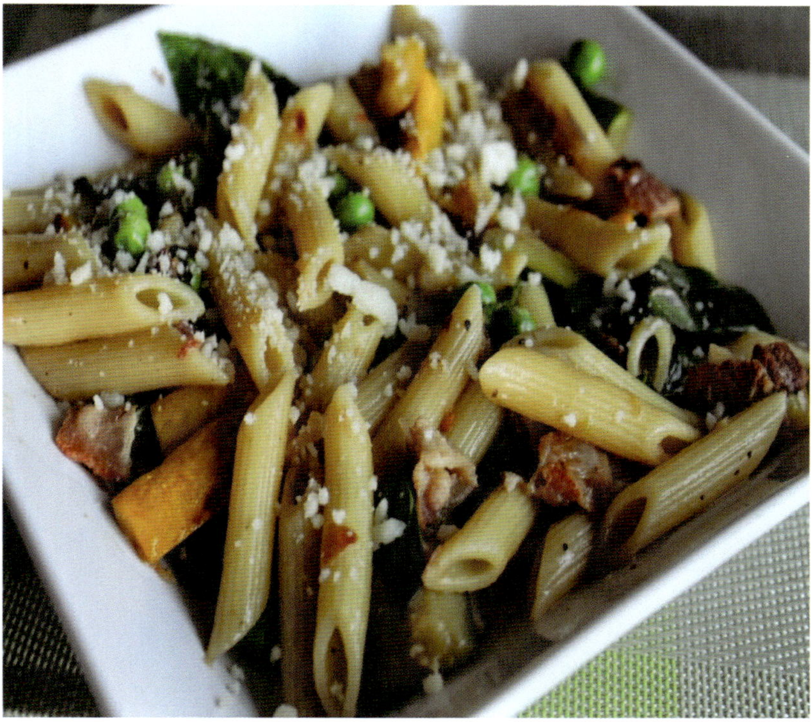

5) Fettuccine with artichokes and shrimp tails

Colorful and tasty this dish combines the delicate flavor of the shrimp, strong taste of artichokes and sweet notes of cherry tomatoes in a riot of scents and aromas. Miss a sprinkling of parsley to also give a fresh touch to this dish making it perfect for your seasonal menu with artichokes.

Preparation: 30 min

Cooking Time: 35 mins

Portions: 4 servings

Ingredients:

- Egg fettuccine 250 g
- Cherry tomatoes 300g
- Artichokes (about 4) 500 g
- Shrimp 250g
- Tomato puree 200 ml
- Extra virgin olive oil 30 g
- Shallot 50 g
- Parsley, chopped 10 g
- Fish soup 150 g
- Lemon juice 1
- Fine salt to taste
- Black pepper to taste

Instructions:

Start the preparation of fettuccine with artichokes and shrimp tails from cleaning the artichokes: eliminate the outer leaves and leathery, taking care to keep soaking the hearts of the artichokes in water acidulated with lemon juice. Cut the tips that have the thorns, then divide in half artichokes and with a corer remove the central beard.

Then, eliminate the most external part of the shank with a potato peeler and cut the stem into small pieces and the sliced artichoke heart. Preserve in water acidulated the chopped artichoke.

The shrimp: Remove the head and the shell, and gently pull out the intestines, setting aside the prawns.

Peel up the shallots and chop them. After that, wash the tomatoes and cut them into wedges. In a pan heat the olive oil, add the chopped shallots and let dry on low heat for 5 minutes. If they are too dry add a tablespoon of fish or water balloon.

When the shallot is wilted, incorporate the artichokes drained water, and add a ladle of vegetable stock, also united the tomatoes, and the tomato sauce. Cook it over medium heat for about 10 minutes and occasionally pour another ladle of stock. Meanwhile, bring to boil a pot full of water and salt (to taste) and add some chopped parsley.

Add the shrimp tails, sauté for 5 minutes then turn off the heat. Pour also the fettuccine in boiling water and cook for about 5-6 minutes, then drain, and pour directly into the pan with the sauce. Toss the noodles in the sauce of artichokes and prawns for flavor and then serve hot.

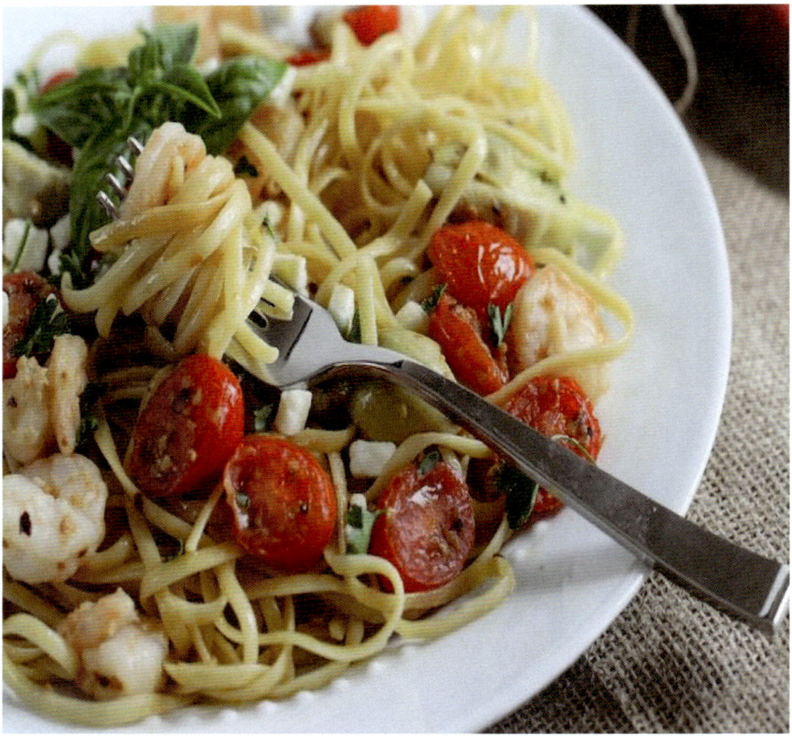

6) Spaghetti aglio, olio e peperoncino

The spaghetti with garlic, olive oil and chili is a simple dish of the Italian cuisine. Despite this simplicity, they are certainly the most popular cooks in households, and in the famous restaurants as well. The spicy taste of peperoncino, the garlic smell and finally the rich quality of the olive oil makes this dish so exquisite. As is considered a simple recipe, we must be careful and rigorously when choosing the ingredients and cautious during the preparation if we want to get an excellent result.

Preparation: 5 min

Cooking time: 10 min

Portions: 4 people

Ingredients:

- 400 g Spaghetti
- 10 g Garlic
- 10 g Fresh spicy red pepper
- 5 tbsp. Extra virgin olive oil
- Salt (to taste)
- 5 g Parsley

Instructions:

Take a high-sided pan, add some water and bring it to a boil. Put the pasta inside and let them cook. Let them cook and move to the sauce: carve the fresh chili peppers lengthwise and remove their seeds. Then cut the resulting pepper into fine strips, and chop the parsley until it gets as mince.

Heat in a large frying pan some olive oil. Add the peeled garlic and the chili peppers and let them fry, until they get a goldish color. After a few minutes, remove the garlic and add two or three spoons of pasta cooking water.

Take out the spaghetti from the boiled water and put them in the pan. Leave it to cook for about 5 minutes more, meanwhile, season it with some chopped parsley. If it's necessary, you can add more cooking water into the pan.

Take the spaghetti out from the pan and place it on a nice plate. Enjoy this nice spaghetti dish!

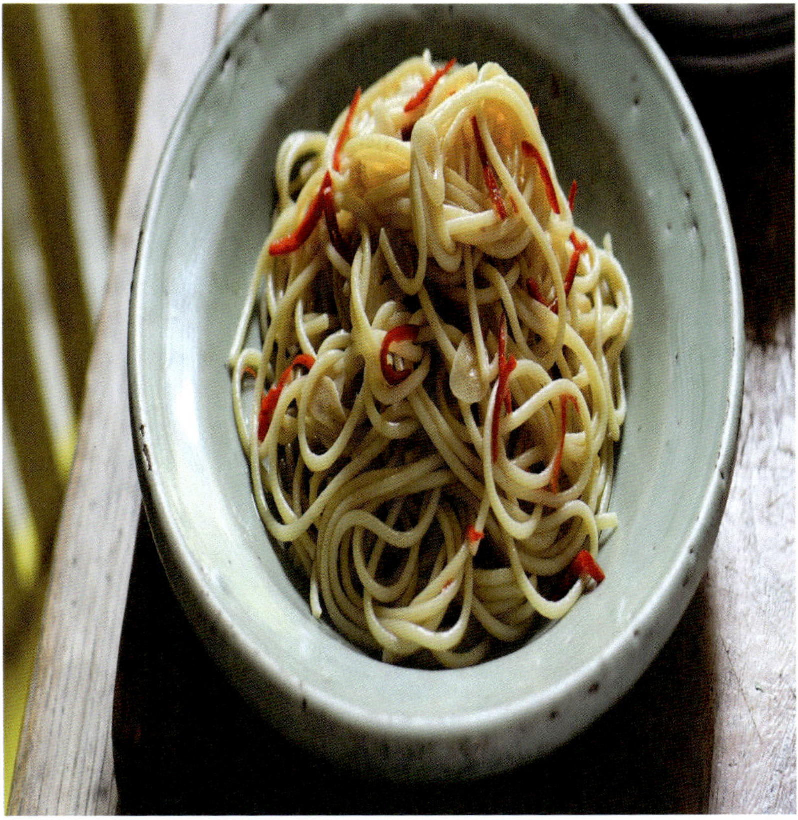

7) Penne all'Arrabbiata

The Penne all'Arrabbiata it's a traditional dish of Lazio. The dish is very famous for this culinary culture, prepared with a few and simple ingredients which have a strong flavor. The sauce for this pasta dish is made with fresh tomatoes, garlic, and chili. In the end, the final touch is the intense flavor of Pecorino. It is often eaten as a late-night snack while gathering home with friends because of its simplicity and the fast cooking.

Their unique angry name derives from the fact that when people are eating chili pens, they tend to get red in the face, and are compared with "angry people."

Preparation: 15 min

Cooking time: 10 min

Portions: 4 people

Ingredients

- 320 g Penne Rigate
- 400 g tomatoes
- 4 tbsp. Extra virgin olive oil
- 2 cloves Garlic
- 5 g Fresh red pepper
- 100 g Roman Pecorino
- Salt and pepper (to taste)

Instructions:

First, start preparing the sauce. Wash the tomatoes carefully and then make an "x" with the knife at the point where the stem was. This kind of chopping allows us to remove the peel quickly from the tomatoes. Take a pan with high sides and put some water to boil in it, and add the tomatoes inside for a few minutes.

Using a skimmer, drain the tomatoes and place them into a bowl with ice and water. Now, you can easily remove the skin and the seeds. Cut the tomatoes into small cubes and place them in a small bowl.

Take the hot pepper and cut it into small strips and take out the seeds inside. Heat in a large frying pan the olive oil. Sauté one of the garlic cloves (or even more, depending on your taste) with the chopped peppers, and mix them until they get a nice brown color. After that add the tomato cubes and make sure to mix continuously to allow a uniform cooking. You can season it with some pepper and salt.

Now, it's time for preparing the pasta. Take a high-sided pan, add some water and bring it to a boil. Put the pasta inside and let them cook. After they are cooked, add them to the sauce pan.

Finally, add the chopped fresh parsley and mix the ingredients well. When you place the pasta in the plate pour some grated pecorino.

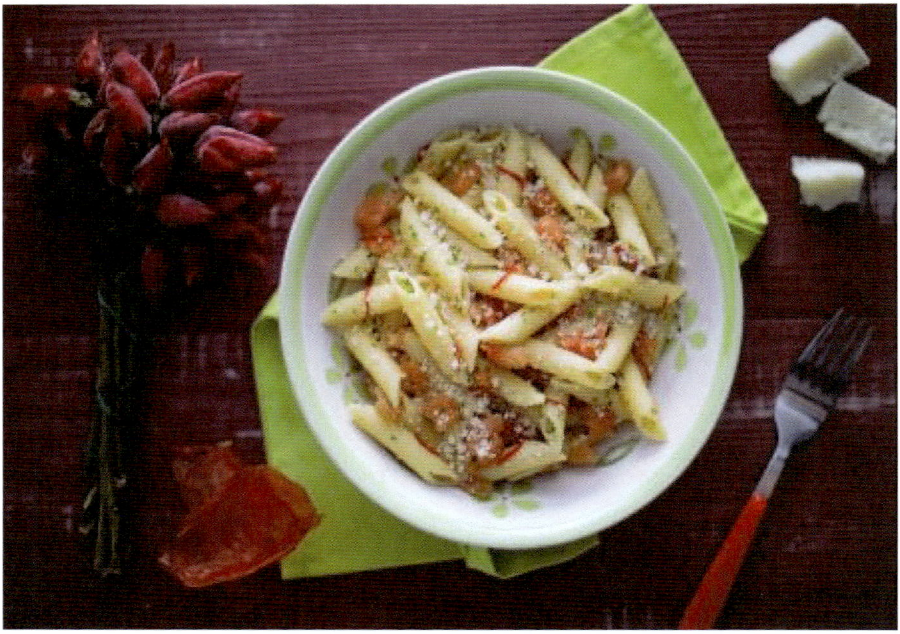

8) Spaghetti col rancetto

The spaghetti with rancetto is one of the most delicious dishes of the Umbrian kitchen. The term "rancetto" comes from the slight flavor of rancid of cured bacon used in the preparation.

This dish stands as a first course and contains the following ingredients: bacon, cheese, fresh tomatoes and marjoram which makes this dish so exquisite. It is recommended to add it at the end of cooking, to keep the freshness and fragrance of the dish.

Preparation: 15 min

Cooking Time: 20 min

Portions: 4 servings

Ingredients:

- 400 g Spaghetti
- 200 g Bacon
- Extra virgin olive oil (to taste)
- 1 White onion
- Marjoram taste
- Pecorino, hard to taste
- Salt (to taste)
- Black pepper (to taste)
- 400 g Peeled tomatoes

Instructions:

First, start by preparing the spaghetti. Take a high-sided pan, add some salted water and bring it to a boil, and later add the pasta. After washing and cutting the onion carefully, put them in a frying pan and drizzle some extra virgin olive oil. Let it dry for 5 minutes and when they get a transparent color, add the bacon (cut into cubes).

After the bacon gets a brown color, add the chopped peeled tomatoes. Cook the ingredients on a low heat for 10 minutes, while adding some salt and pepper seasonings, according to your taste.

Take the spaghetti, drain them, and move them into the saucepan. Add the fresh marjoram and let it cook for a few minutes more. Serve this nice dish with grated Pecorino and rancetto.

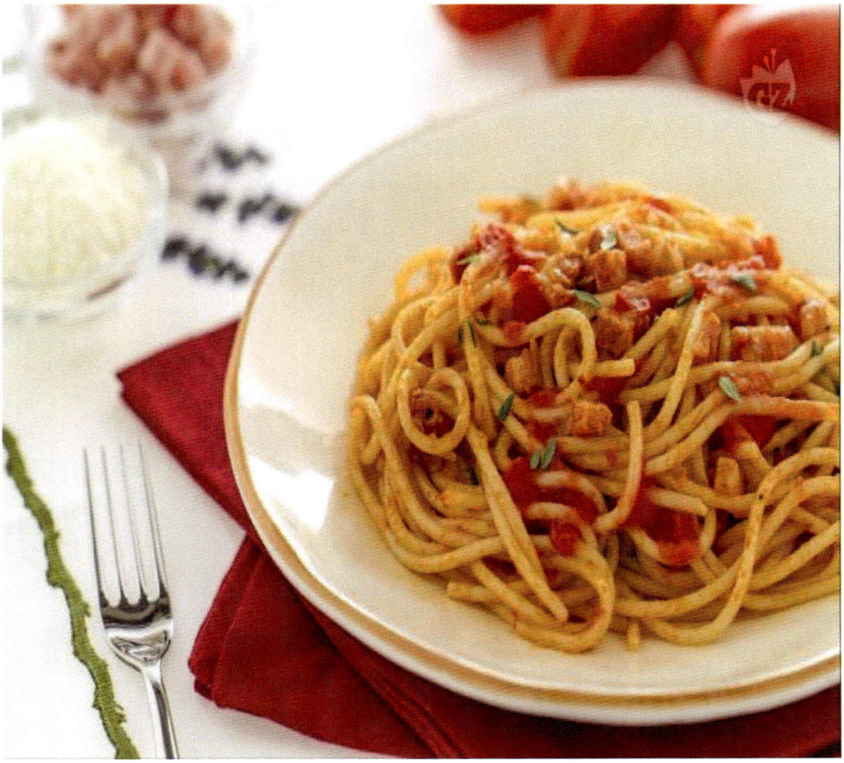

9) Tagliatelle con pesto di salvia

Tagliatelle con pesto di salvia recipe it's originally from Liguria and its flavor its unique. The tagliatelle con pesto di salvia contains the following ingredients: fresh basil leaves, bacon, garlic, and hazelnuts. This combination of ingredients will make your mouth melt down.

This recipe needs to be prepared gently, and you should not heat so much the raw ingredients. The pesto sauce is used for seasoning the long pasta such as spaghetti or the short pasta such as trofie. The traditional version of the recipe also includes green beans and potatoes.

Preparation: 15 min

Cooking Time: 20 mins

Portions: 4 servings

Ingredients:

- 400 g of Fresh noodles
- 15 Sage leaves
- 50 g Toasted hazelnuts
- 20 g Romano Pecorino
- 2 slices of bacon (to taste)
- 4 tbsp. of Extra virgin olive oil
- Salt (to taste)
- Pepper (to taste)

Instructions:

Start this dish with washing the 15 sage leaves. Mix them into a bowl with the hazelnuts, pecorino, olive oil, and season it with salt and pepper.

Take a frying pan and bake 2 slices of chopped bacon in it, without seasoning them. After they get a brown color take the bacon and dry them on paper towels.

Now, start cooking the fresh noodles in a boiling salted water. After 10 minutes take them out from the water and drain them well. Add the pasta on a plate, dress it with the pesto previously prepared, and finally, add the bacon. Enjoy this nice and delicious spaghetti dish!

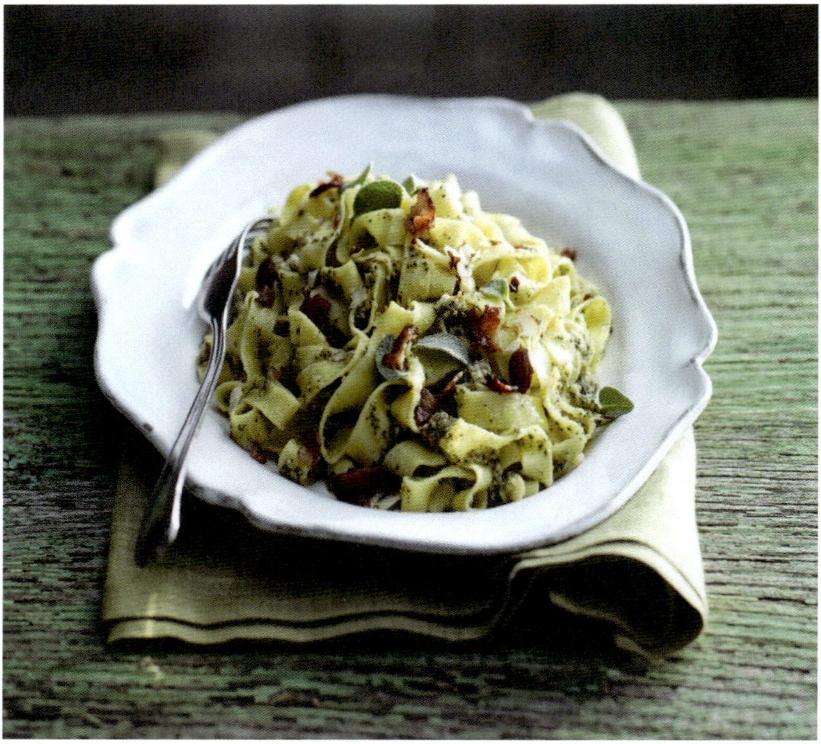

10) Spaghetti alla puttanesca

Spaghetti alla puttanesca is the most demanded and appreciated by the tourists that visit Italy. Within this dish, they will find a nice mix of flavors of the Italian cuisine. The ingredients that are contained in this recipe are fresh tomatoes and olives, capers and a rich flavor of hot pepper and parsley.

Some people say that this recipe was created a long time ago for attracting customers, with this quick and tasty cook. The main region from where this dish comes is Lazio and Campania.

Preparation: 15 min

Cooking Time: 15 mins

Portions: 4 servings

Ingredients:

- 400g Spaghetti
- 100 g Black olives
- 1 tbsp. Capers under salt
- 500 g of Peeled Tomatoes
- 2 cloves of Garlic
- 2 tbsp. chopped Parsley
- 5 tbsp. Extra virgin olive oil
- Fine salt (to taste)
- Fresh red pepper (to taste)
- 8 Sardines salted fillets

Instructions:

Wash the tomatoes carefully and then make an "x" with the knife at the point where the stem was and put them in boiling water for 1-2 minutes. Then take them out from water and now you can easily peel them. Remove the seeds from the tomatoes and then cut them into small cubes.

Now, wash the anchovies and the capers, and then dry them well. Cut them into small pieces, and move them into a small bowl. Inside the bowl cut the garlic, the black olives.

Take a frying pan, and heat some extra virgin olive oil, add the other garlic clove and cook for 1 minute. After that, add the mixed ingredients from the bowl and let the anchovies melt in the chili flavor. You can also add the tomatoes and some parsley in a few minutes.

Meantime, take the pasta and build them into salted water for about 10 minutes. After the pasta is well cooked, take it out, drain them well and add them inside the frying pan on the sauce. Cook them for about two minutes more.

The spaghetti alla puttanesca are ready to be served!

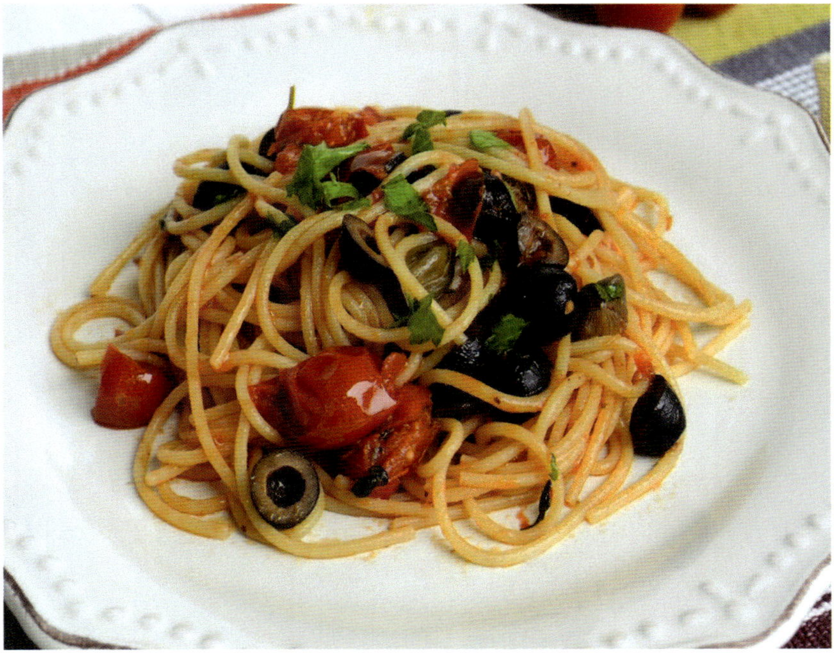

11) Spaghetti cacio e pepe

The spaghetti with cheese and pepper are a particularity of the Roman tradition. Within this recipe are used only a few ingredients: Pecorino Romano joined in a creamy sauce with the pepper. Don't think that this dish might be boring, because the ingredients used are of a highest quality, and give this recipe a delicious flavor.

This recipe's often cooked late night while gathering with friends because of its simplicity and rapidness. After tasting this kind of dish, your mouth will melt instantaneously.

Preparation: 10 min

Cooking Time: 10 mins

Portions: 4 servings

Ingredients:

- 320 g Spaghetti
- Black pepper (to taste)
- 160 g Roman Pecorino (for grating)
- 1 pinch of Fine salt

Instructions:

To prepare spaghetti with cheese and pepper take a high-sided pan and boil the pasta in the salted water.

During the preparation of pasta, we can start making the sauce: pour the grated Pecorino Romano in a large bowl and add some boiled water from the pasta. Easily mix the cheese until it will get creamy and smooth, and add some black pepper.

When the pasta are cooked, drain them and put them inside the bowl. Mix well the pasta with the creamy paste. If you notice that you need more Pecorino or water, you can adjust it, just be sure that the composition it's not dry. Once the spaghetti is mixed, place them on a plate and pour some more ground pepper (to taste). The cheeses spaghetti and pepper are to be served immediately!

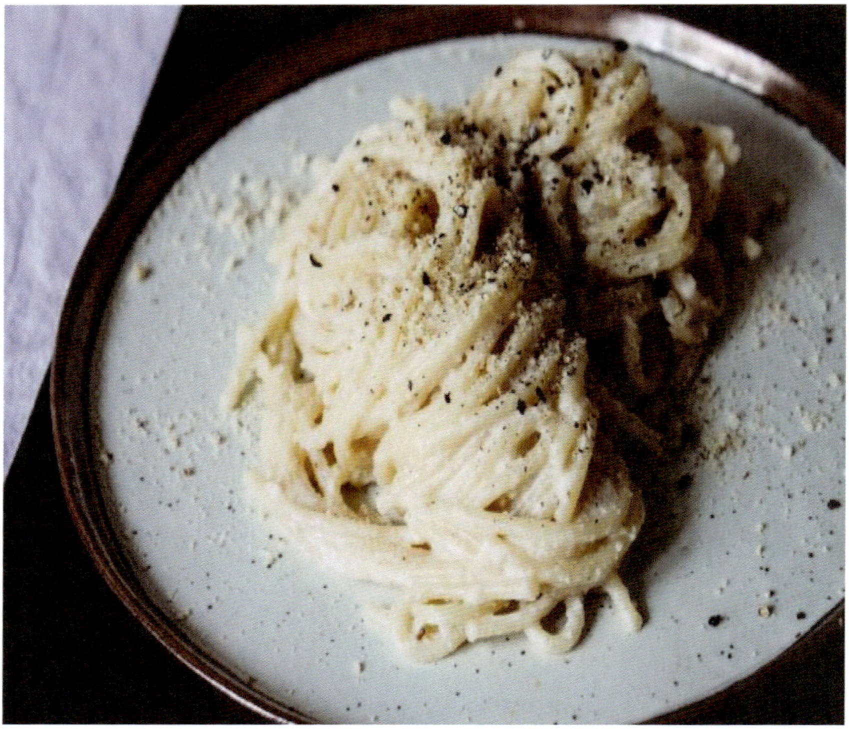

12) Pasta con ragù ai funghi

The pasta con ragu ai funghi is a first simple and delicious dish that can be perfectly served at every opportunity.

Preparation: 20 min

Cooking Time: 15 mins

Portions: 4 servings

Ingredients:

- 400 g of Peeled Tomatoes
- 360 g of Semolina pasta
- 300 g Veal roast
- 40 g Grit
- 30 g Dried mushrooms
- 2 Shallots
- 5 tbsp. of Extra virgin olive oil
- Salt (to taste)
- Pepper (to taste)

Instructions:

Soak the dried mushrooms in a bowl with hot water and leave it for about 10 minutes, then drain them. Meanwhile, cut the calf into small pieces.

Heat in a frying pan with a little of olive oil those two shallots. After a minute add the mushrooms, the peeled tomatoes and the chopped meat, and let it cook for some minutes. You can season it with some pepper and salt, to your taste.

Prepare the pasta in boiling salted water, and when they are cooked, place them into the sauce. Finally, pour the Parmesan cheese and serve the pasta con ragù ai Funghi!

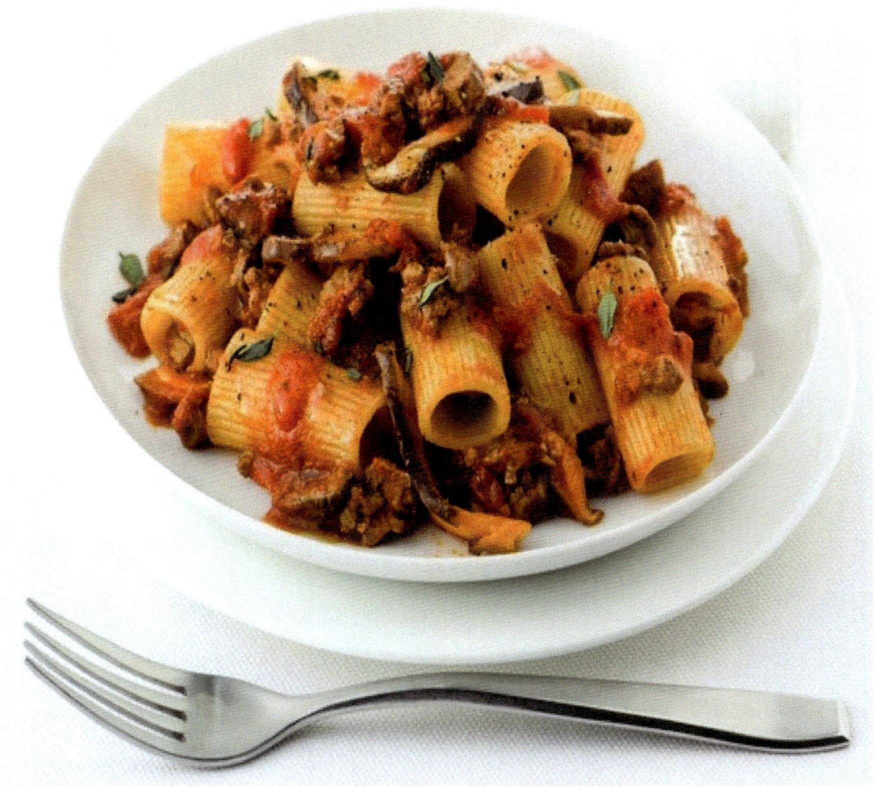

13) Spaghetti alle vongole

Spaghetti alle vongole are very popular along the coast of Italy. Vongole veracity (shell clams) are the special ingredients of this dish. Over the clams, it's added a delicious sauce made with olive oil, garlic, and some chili. Some people prefer the tomato-based version of the sauce.

Preparation: 15 min

Cooking Time: 20 mins

Portions: 4 servings

Ingredients:

- 320 g Spaghetti
- 1 kg Clams
- 1 Garlic clove
- 1 bunch of Parsley
- 4 tbsp. of Extra virgin olive oil
- Black pepper (to taste)
- Fine salt (to taste)
- Rock Salt (to taste the clams

Instructions:

To prepare spaghetti with clams, begin with cleaning the clams. Make sure there are no broken or empty shells if so, discard them. Carefully wash them, because it might contain sand inside. Place them in a large bowl filled with salt and let it marinate for 15 minutes. Also, start cooking the pasta boiling it in salted water.

Take a frying pan and heat some olive oil with garlic. After a few minutes add the clams. The clams will open as they heat up. Once they are opened turn off the heat to avoid them bake too. Collect the juice left by the clams and the garlic and discard them.

After the spaghetti are cooked transfer them over the clams and sauce and season it with some pepper and salt. Finally, add some chopped parsley and serve the spaghetti with clams!

0

14) Spaghetti Fagioli e cozze

The spaghetti with beans and mussels is a dish that combines the flavors of "the earth and the sea." This classical combination it's part of the Bell kitchen, but also enjoyed in other Italian regions.

In this recipe, we are going to use the cannellini beans, one of the most delicate beans. The sauce that we will make, combined with fried clams will give you a delicious taste of flavors. You can adjust the recipe as you like, adding a tomato sauce instead.

Preparation: 15 min

Cooking Time: 15 mins

Portions: 4 servings

Ingredients:

- 320 g Spaghetti
- 1 kg Mussels
- 250 g Precooked cannellini beans
- ½ cup of White wine
- 1 Garlic clove
- 1 Fresh red pepper
- Parsley (to taste)
- Extra virgin olive oil (to taste)
- Fine salt (to taste)
- Black pepper (to taste)

Instructions:

To prepare spaghetti with beans and mussels, start to prepare the mixture for the sauce. Carefully wash and chop the parsley, then peel the garlic clove and chop it, and then cut the chili, removing their seeds.

Take a large pan and put some olive oil, add the garlic, chili, and some chopped parsley and let them fry on low heat, stirring occasionally.

Meanwhile, take the mussels and clean them under running water. Eliminate the fine of the mussels and rub the surface with a sharp knife. Rinse them and transfer them into the pan with a sauce that you've prepared lately. Pour the white wine and let it evaporate for a few moments, covering the pan with a lid. Leave it for a few minutes more, then stop the heat and leave the mussels to take the flavor.

After a few minutes, start the heat again, and you can add the cannellini beans, and season the sauce with some pepper and salt. Let them cook for about 3-4 minutes until the beans are softened.

Meanwhile, start cooking the pasta in boiling salted water for 5 minutes. Then, drain them and transfer them directly into the pan with mussels and beans. Add the remaining chopped parsley, stir and serve this delicious spaghetti with beans and mussels!

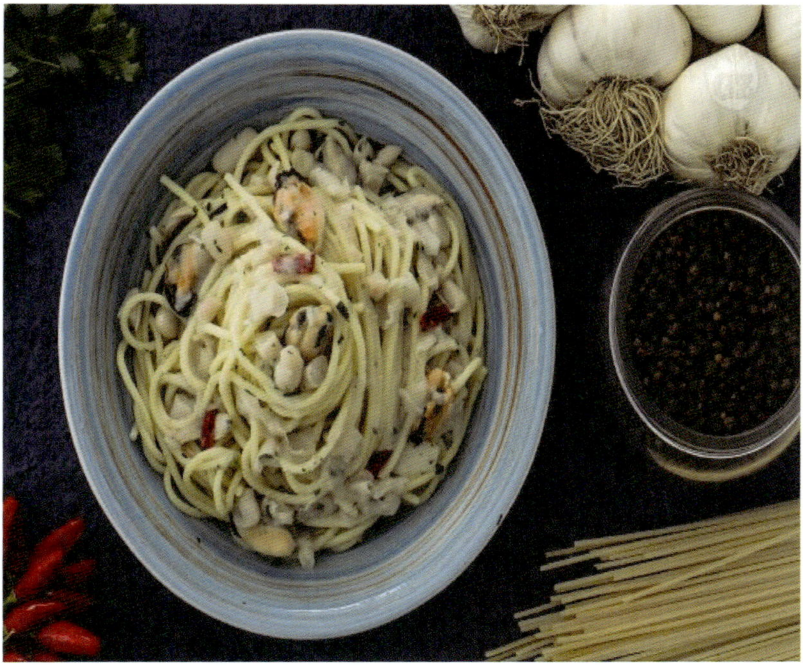

15) Pasta al verde con gamberetti

Pasta al verde con ganberetti looks like pesto, but it is not! This pasta with green shrimp is a dish that combines a delicious vegetable sauce and tasty shrimp stir-fried. The green paste it's made by mixing the asparagus and spinach, and the other ingredients: almonds and pine nuts. As it's a starting course, it can be eaten cold, maybe when going out for picnics. If you don't have asparagus, you can use some chopped zucchini instead, and you will get still a good pasta!

Preparation: 20 min

Cooking Time: 15 mins

Portions: 4 servings

Ingredients:

- 320 g Fusilli
- 300 g Shrimps
- 20 ml White wine
- Extra virgin olive oil (to taste)
- **For the green sauce**
- 200 g Asparagus
- 100 g Spinach
- 30 g Pine nuts
- 30 g Almond peeled
- 5 tbsp. of Extra virgin olive oil
- 30 g Pecorino (to be grated)
- 30 g Grana Padano (to be grated)
- ½ Garlic clove

Instructions:

To prepare the green sauce with shrimp, start by washing the asparagus and cut the part of the stem. Boil the asparagus in the high-sided pan, leaving the emerged points. When they are cooked, immediately transfer them into a bowl filled with ice. That's done for keeping the color of asparagus intact. Then cut them and put them aside.

Next, put the washed spinach and asparagus in a mixer, and also add the peeled almonds and pine nuts. Also, add a half clove of garlic, some olive oil, and the grated cheese. Blend the ingredients together, until you get a nice creamy paste and keep it aside.

Continue with the preparation of the shrimp. Pull off the head, remove its shell and put it into a frying pan. Add some olive oil and heat it up. Season it with some pepper and salt, and add the white wine to give the Shrimps a nice flavor. Cook and stir for a few minutes, until the shrimps will get a brown color.

Put the pasta to boil into salted water for about 5 minutes, while in the pan pour the mixed green sauce. Add some cooking water and when the pasta are cooked, drain them and transfer them into the pan. Cook a few minutes more, adding some seasoning (salt and pepper). Turn off the heat and your pasta with shrimp will be ready!

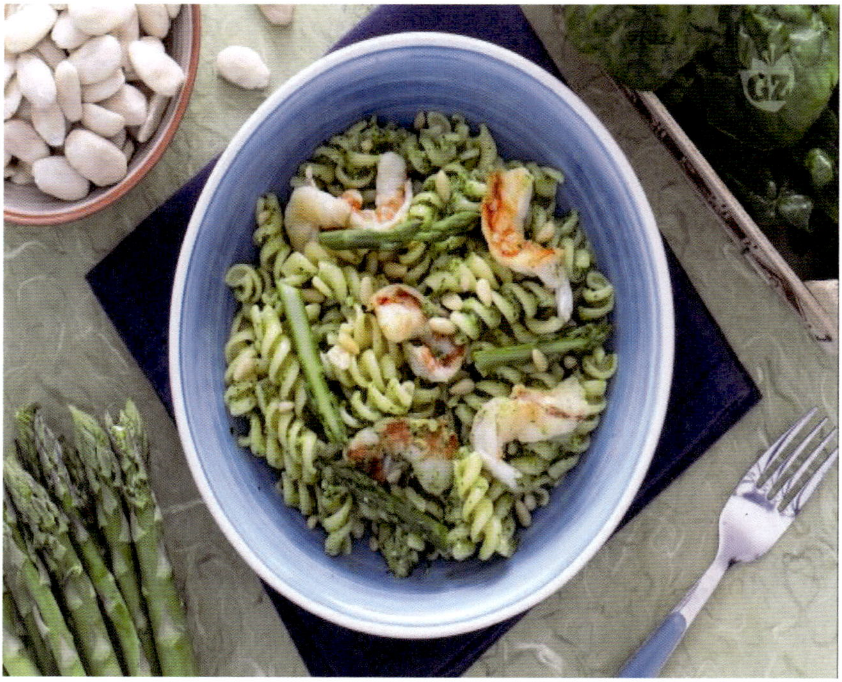

16) Rigatoni con carciofi, olive e capperi

The rigatoni with artichokes, olives, and capers is a quick and easy dish to prepare, full of flavors. Artichokes can be easily transformed in a tasty and delicious sauce and combined with anchovies and capers, the two Mediterranean ingredients. This first course is ideal for dinners, especially when gathering with your friends, and you want to make a good impression.

Preparation: 20 min

Cooking Time: 15 mins

Portions: 4 servings

Ingredients:

- 320 g Rigatoni
- 6 Artichokes
- 200 g Olives (pitted)
- 35 g Anchovies (anchovies)
- 30 g Capers (under salt)
- 100 ml White wine
- 3 tbsp. of Extra virgin olive oil
- 2 Garlic cloves
- Fine salt (to taste)
- Black pepper (to taste)
- 3 Thyme sprigs

Instructions:

To prepare this dish start with chopping the artichokes, but before touching protect your hands with gloves or rub the skin with lemon, to avoid getting black. Remove the outer leaves with a sharp knife. Cut together the top and the back part of the shank. Peel the stems, eliminate the filamentous, and cut it into cubes. Transfer them into a bowl filled with water and lemon, for preventing discoloration.

Cut the artichoke top hearts into quarters and add them in the water bowl. Take a frying pan, pour some olive oil and let it heat. After a minute, add the garlic and transfer the artichokes from the water inside the pan. Season the ingredients with some pepper and salt, and also pour the wine over them. After 5 minutes of cooking add the pitted olives, and mix the ingredients from the pan together.

Chop the anchovies and capers and then place them with the artichokes and cook for another 5 minutes. Take off the pan from the heat and leave it aside.

Start cooking the pasta boiled in salted water for 5 minutes. After they are cooked, drain them and add them to the sauce and stir with a large spoon. If necessary, you can add a little of cooking water. Your rigatoni with artichokes, olives, and capers are ready to serve!

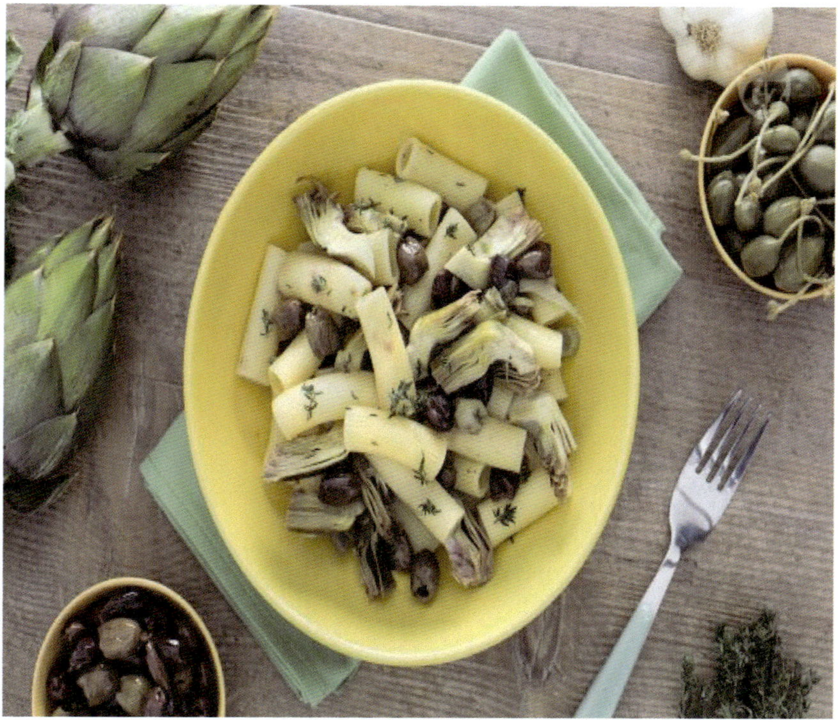

17) Spaghetti al Tonno

Imagine that you are coming home after work and you didn't do any shopping, and you're wondering what to eat now. But, then you find on the shelf some tuna in oil. That's how this tasty spaghetti with tuna recipe begins. It's an easy and perfect dish to prepare, which can save your dinner with his simplest ingredients. Choose a meaty tuna, a fresh bunch of parsley and a little of extra virgin olive oil to flavor this dish. Also, add a pinch of butter to give the recipe a creamy taste.

Preparation: 5 min

Cooking Time: 10 mins

Portions: 4 servings

Ingredients:

- 320 g Tuna in oil
- 30 g Butter
- 10 g Extra virgin olive oil
- Parsley (to taste)
- Fine salt (to taste)
- Black pepper (to taste)

Instructions:

Start preparing the spaghetti with tuna by draining the tuna from the oil retention (you will have like 200 g of tuna). Take the parsley and pull his leaves from the twigs off and chop them.

Then, you can start boiling the pasta in salted water for 10 minutes. While the pasta it's cooking, start doing the sauce. Cut the butter into four pieces and throw them into a heated pan. Add some olive oil and the fresh tuna into the pan and let it cook for about 4 minutes.

Take out the pasta from the water, drain it and move it into the pan, also add some water. Mix the fresh tuna for about 1 minute, and add salt and pepper during this time.

In the end, season the dish with chopped parsley. Your spaghetti with tuna is now ready for the plate!

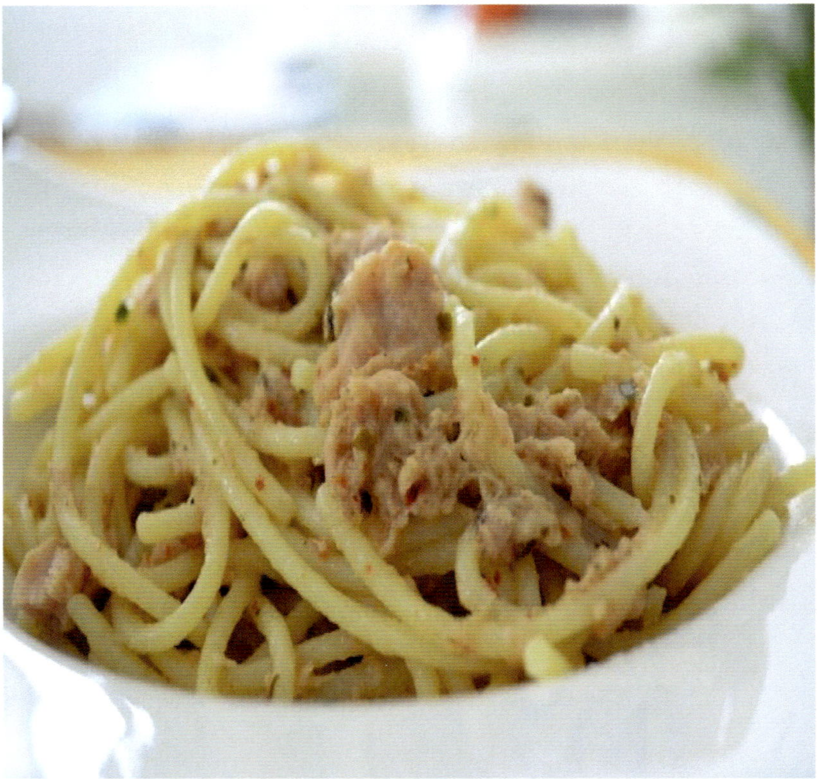

18) Pasta al gorgonzola gratinata al forno

Fruity, soft and seductive, the gorgonzola is the king of the Italian cuisine with its unique flavor and distinctive aroma. Very versatile, it can be a perfect to give an intense note of taste to appetizers or irresistible creams accompanying dishes of risotto or pasta. We suggest this nice dish of pasta with gorgonzola while spending some time with your friends. You can easily surprise them with this delicious recipe!

The cellentani are used to absorb the flavor of the gorgonzola, and the walnuts give a crunchy taste. They are made in the oven, and this gives the pasta a delicious golden crust.

Preparation: 10 min

Cooking Time: 10 mins

Portions: 4 servings

Ingredients:

- 320 g Cellentani
- 300 g Gorgonzola
- 50 g Walnuts
- 50 ml Whole milk
- 50 g Grana Padano (grated)

Instructions:

First, start with boiling the pasta into salted water for about 10 minutes.

Take the gorgonzola cheese and cut it into small cubes; do this with the walnuts. In a frying pan add the milk and gorgonzola and let it melt, until it gets a creamy look. After two or three minutes the cream will be finished. Once the pasta it's done, drain it and transfer it into the pan, over the sauce and mix it well.

Place the pan composition in a high-side rectangular cooking tray and pour over the Grana and the walnuts. Cook for five minutes in the oven on the grill mode. Your pasta with gorgonzola au gratin is ready to be served!

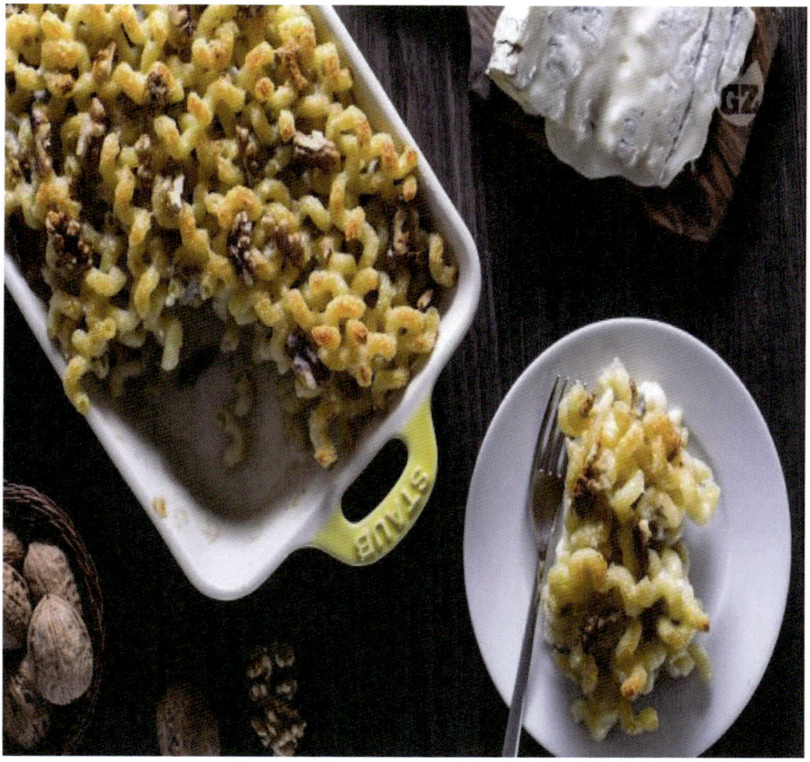
STAUB

19) Pasta radicchio e zola

Within this dish, the combination of radicchio and zola (gorgonzola) go very well, thanks to the rich taste that characterizes them.

In this cookbook, we combined them together to make a delicious radicchio and gorgonzola pasta as a main course. You can use spicy or sweet gorgonzola to customize this recipe, which fits for any pasta. We used the gluten-free penne that can better absorb the sauce and make this dish also suitable for those who are intolerant to gluten. For decorating the plate, you can pour some chopped walnuts over the pasta, adding a unique flavor to it.

Preparation: 20 min

Cooking Time: 22 mins

Portions: 4 servings

Ingredients:

- 320 g Penne Rigate Gluten Free
- 460 g Radicchio
- 250 g Gorgonzola
- 80 g Walnuts
- 100 g Fresh cream
- Fine salt (to taste)

- Black pepper (to taste)
- 2 tbsp. of Extra virgin olive oil
- 20 ml Water
- 1 Garlic clove

Instructions:

Start preparing the radicchio and gorgonzola pasta by putting the penne to boil under sated water.

During the cooking the pasta, you can take the radicchio and clean it: cut the hardest part from the end and browse it, then wash the leaves carefully and cut them into strips. At this point, you can switch to Zola, by eliminating the outer crust of it and cut it into cubes. Pour the fresh cream into a saucepan and heat it for a minute. Add the zola and let it melt slowly, mixing occasionally.

Take a frying pan, put some olive oil and garlic on the heat. Add the chopped radicchio and some water, and leave them for a few minutes. Take out the garlic and pour the cream with zola over the radicchio and mix them occasionally.

Using a knife chop the walnuts coarsely. Drain the cooked pasta and put it in the frying pan. Add the walnuts, salt, pepper and wait for 1-2 minutes. Serve the pasta with radicchio and gorgonzola while it's still hot!

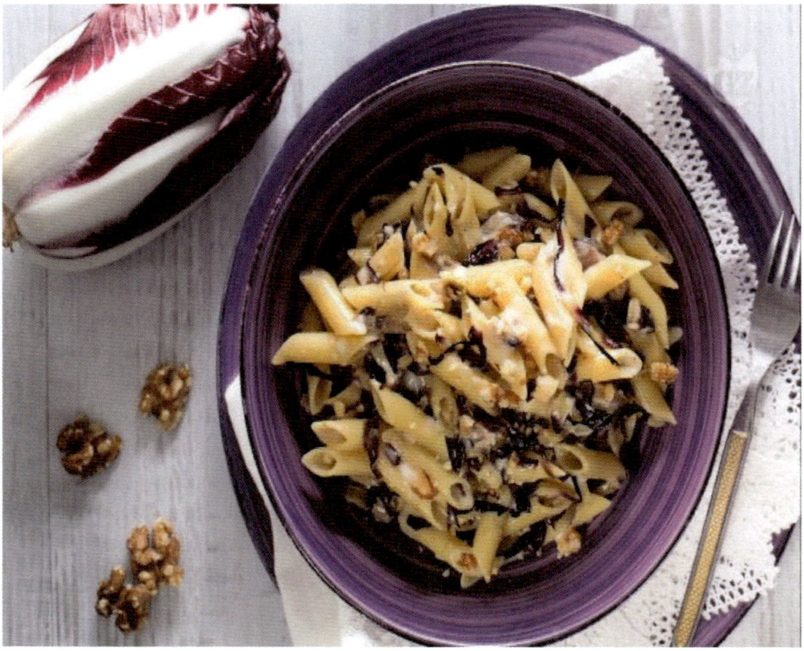

20) Tonnarelli al pesto di rucola

The tonnarelli with rucola pesto are a very simple dish to prepare. You can easily blend a few ingredients like fresh rucola, pine nuts, olive oil and parmesan to get a nice cream full of flavors in just a few minutes.

The tonnarelli pasta is also called spaghetti alla chitarra, because of their look and the well-suited sauces: from the mushrooms and tomatoes, from the clams which are the most delicious one.

This version with rucola pesto has a light taste, where the rocket is balanced by pine nuts and cheese.

Preparation: 15 min

Cooking Time: 15 mins

Portions: 4 servings

Ingredients:

Ingredients

- 500 g Spaghetti

Ingredients for the rocket pesto

- 100 g Rocket
- 50 g Pine nuts
- 1 Garlic clove
- 5 g Climbs

- 50 g fresh Parmigiano-Reggiano (grated)
- Extra virgin olive oil (to taste)

Instructions:

To prepare tonnarelli arugula pesto, start with boiling the pasta into salted water.

Prepare the pesto: after washing and drying well the rocket, move it into a mixer. Also, you need to add the garlic, pine nuts, a bit of olive oil, parmesan and some salt.

Mix the ingredients well, and during this process add continuously olive oil, until it gets a creamy consistency. When the mixed paste it's ready put it in a pan and heat the cream. After a few minutes, you will have to add the drained pasta and cook it for 2 minutes

Your tonnarelli rucola pesto are ready to be served!

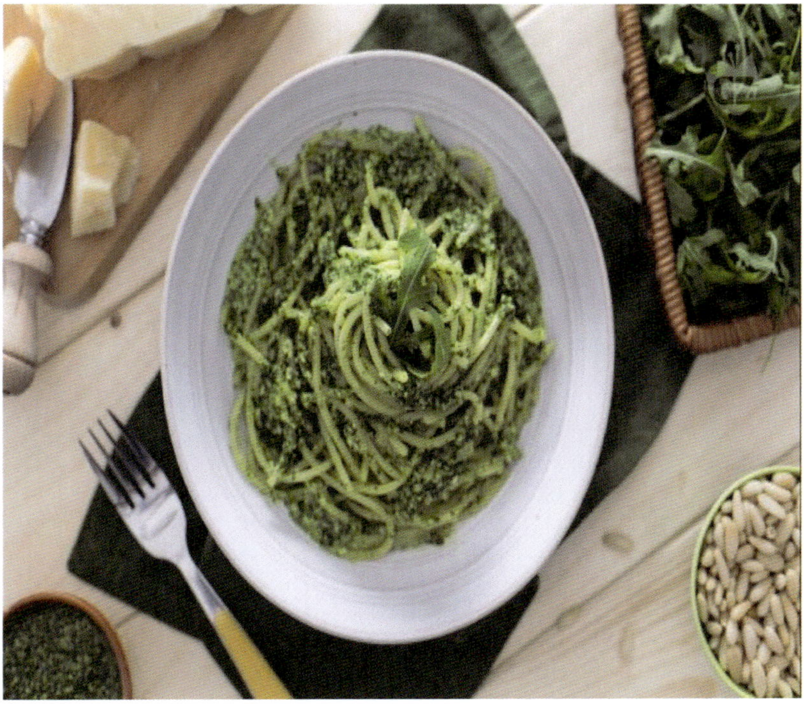

Chapter 2: Vegetarian Pasta dishes

1) Pasta con le melanzane

Pasta with eggplant is a colorful vegetarian dish, which can be made very quick and easily. The dish contains Mediterranean ingredients, which give a balance in freshness: the delicious cherry tomatoes and fresh basil leaves. It can be served either cold, either warm!

Preparation: 15 min

Cooking Time: 20 mins

Portions: 4 servings

Ingredients:

- 320 g Sedanini Rigati
- 350 g Eggplant
- 250 g Cherry tomatoes
- Basil leaves
- 100 g Fresh Onion
- Salt (to taste)
- Black pepper (to taste)
- 3 tbsp. Extra virgin olive oil

Instructions:

To prepare Pasta con le melanzane, start by cutting the Eggplant into small cubes of approximately 1 cm. Put them aside in a colander seasoning them with some salt, and let them drain for 10 minutes.

Meanwhile, cut the onion in thin slices and together with some olive oil put them into a frying pan to heat. After the onion slices get well browned, add the eggplant, season it with some pepper and salt and let it cook for about 10 minutes.

Wash the tomatoes and cut them into quarters and add them to the cooked eggplant.

Start preparing the pasta, by boiling them in salted water for 5 minutes. Drain them, and transfer them into the frying pan. Pour the basil leaves, and your pasta con le melanzane is now ready!

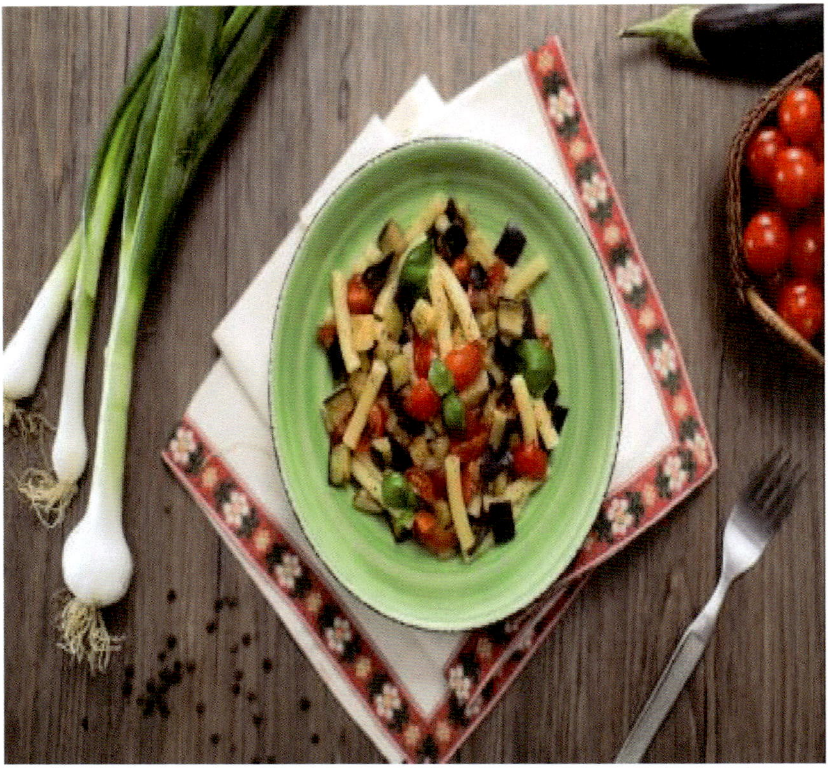

2) Pasta alla carrettiera

The pasta alla carrettiera is a first very delicious and tasty dish made with a few and simple ingredients. Their name come from the Sicilian carters. The dish can be preserved for hours or even days.

The recipe has got different versions, and it's available in the Roman cuisine. Other versions also have, mushrooms and tuna. Within this recipe, we dress it with chili, garlic, and raw parsley.

Preparation: 15 min

Cooking Time: 8 mins

Portions: 4 servings

Ingredients:

- 320 g Spaghetti
- 150 g Pecorino (grated)
- 1 sprig of Parsley
- 1 Fresh red pepper
- 1 Garlic clove
- Extra virgin olive oil (to taste)
- Rock Salt (to taste)

Instructions:

To prepare pasta alla carrettiera, start cooking the pasta boiling it over salted water for 10 minutes. Chop the sprig of parsley and the chili, peel the garlic clove and put the ingredients in a large bowl, adding some olive oil. Season the ingredients with some pepper and salt.

Take the cooked pasta, drain it, and transfer it to the bowl over the mixed ingredients. Add some boiling water, some grated pecorino, chopped parsley and stir if necessary. You can serve pasta alla carrettiera now!

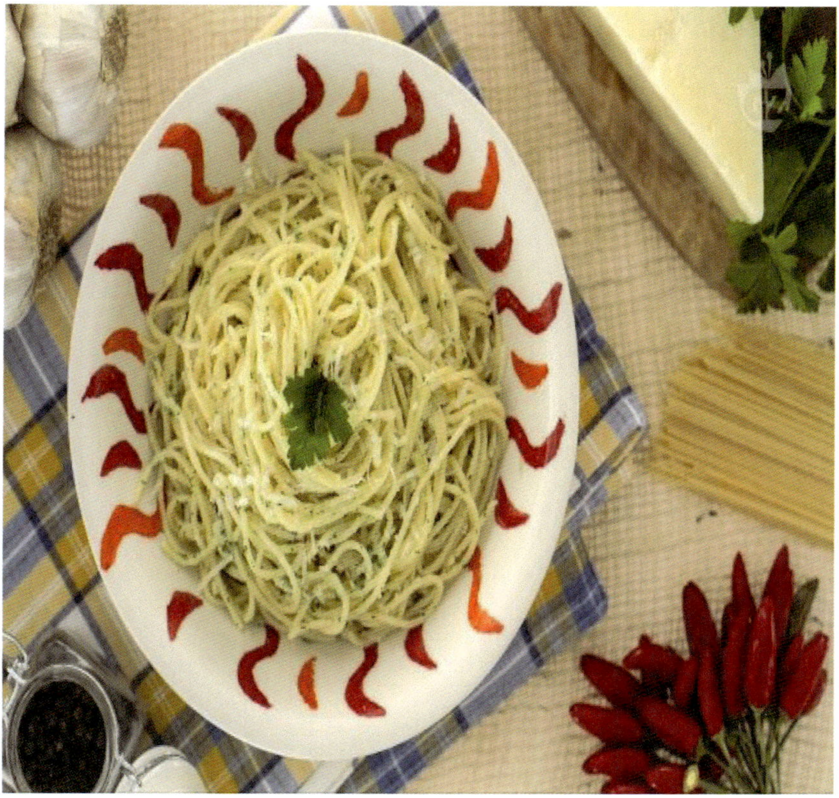

3) Pasta coi fagiolini

Pasta coi fagiolini is a vegetarian dish containing special vegetables: green beans, which are symbolic for summer and suitable for their versatility, for making a delicious and tasty dish.

The bucatini combined with green beans are just the perfect taste of summer. Whether in the mountains, at sea, or you are just home, you should definitely try the pasta with beans!

Preparation: 15 min

Cooking Time: 20 mins

Portions: 4 servings

Ingredients:

- 400 g Bucatini
- 400 g Green beans
- Black pepper (to taste)
- 1 pinch of Salt
- 500 g Tomato puree
- 35 g Shallot
- 3 tbsp. Extra virgin olive oil

Instructions:

To prepare pasta coi fagiolini, start by preparing the sauce: Chop the shallot finely and pour it into a frying pan and add some olive oil. Cook for 2 minutes over a gentle heat, then add the tomato puree. Season with some pepper and salt and let it cook for about 10 minutes

Meanwhile, wash the beans and remove the two ends of them. Pour the beans in some boiling salted water and simmer for two or three minutes. Add the pasta together with the beans and cook for another 5 minutes together.

After you drained the beans and the pasta pour them into the frying pan with the tomato sauce, and mix the ingredients together. You can serve the pasta coi fagiolini now!

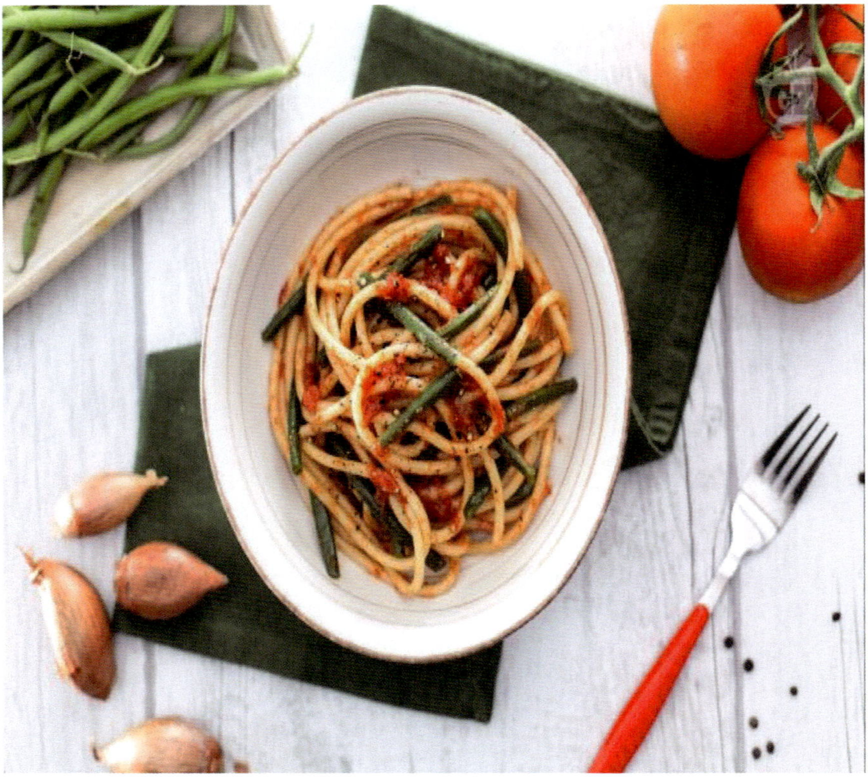

4) Pasta e ricotta

Pasta e ricotta is a delicious and tasty main dish, prepared within few minutes, and it's considered ideal for dinner and lunch. It includes simple and few ingredients, but the most important thing is that ricotta to be fresh. The seasoning with thyme and parmesan gives the recipe a touching flavor and an irresistible freshness.

You can also try to add pappardelle with sautéed zucchini and cream cheese with orange if you look for an alternative version of the dish.

Preparation: 10 min

Cooking Time: 15 mins

Portions: 4 servings

Ingredients:

- 320 g Fusilli
- 350 g Ricotta
- 70 g Parmigiano (grated)
- 70 g of Fresh cream
- Salt (to taste)
- Black pepper (to taste)
- Thyme (to taste)

Instructions:

To prepare pasta e ricotta, start cooking the pasta under boiling salted water for 10 minutes.

Meanwhile, prepare the dressing: Sift the ricotta cheese in a large bowl through a narrow strainer mesh to obtain a nice texture. Add the grated Parmigiano and the fresh cream, and mix them well with a spatula. Pour the thyme leaves, and season with some pepper and salt.

Take the cooked pasta, drain them and transfer them to the bowl with the ricotta mixture. Stir well to mix the sauce with pasta, and add some boiled water if necessary. Your pasta e ricotta is now ready to be served!

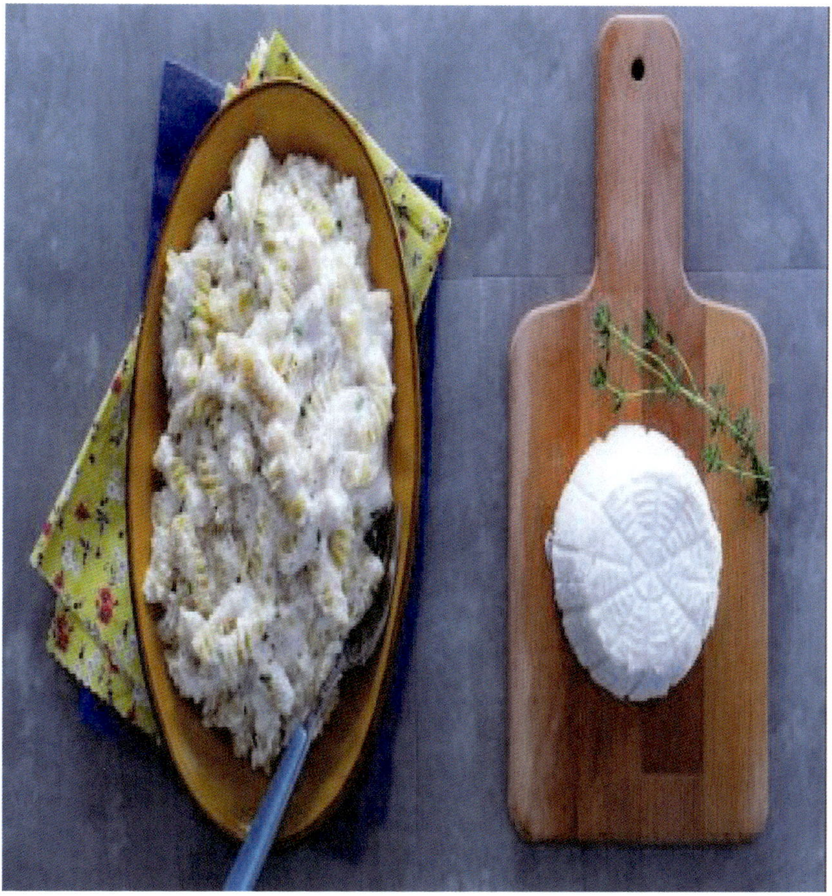

5) Pasta alla checca

The pasta alla checca is a traditional Roman dish, served either warm, either cold. It's the perfect recipe for summer, full of irresistible flavors. In this recipe, we changed the classic recipe, by adding the burrata and mozzarella.

Preparation: 15 min

Cooking Time: 12 mins

Portions: 4 servings

Ingredients:

- 320 g Sedanini Rigati
- 350 g Cherry tomatoes
- 200 g Burrata
- 200 g Caciotta Romano
- 3 g Sale until
- 1 g Black pepper
- Basil (to taste)
- 4 tbsp. Extra virgin olive oil

Instructions:

To prepare the pasta with checca, first, start cooking the pasta under boiling salted water. When pasta already cooked, drain the pasta and transfer into a bowl, pour some olive oil over to keep from sticking together.

Take the burrata and cut it into strips and the Roman Caciotta into cubes. Carefully wash the tomatoes under running cold water and cut them into quarters. Add them to the pasta, chop some basil over, and season with some pepper and salt. Your pasta alla checca is ready to be enjoyed!

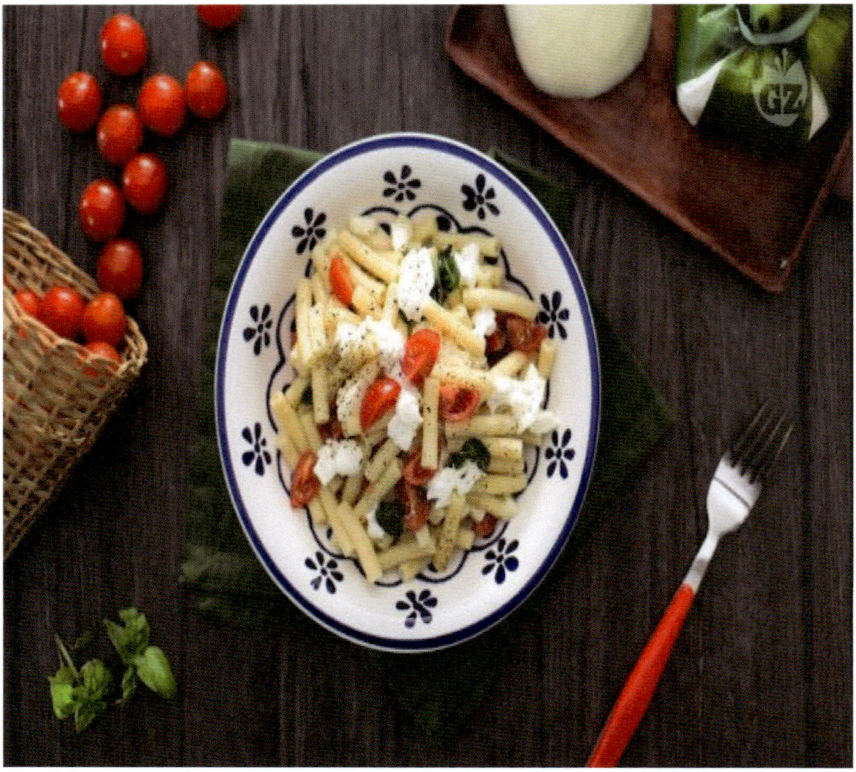

Conclusion

The Italian cuisine has developed during the centuries of political and social changes, with roots stretching to antiquity. During the discovery of tomatoes, potatoes, bell peppers and maize the Italian cuisine gained significant diversity and originality. There is also a big difference between the north part of the Italy and the proper peninsula in taste, because of the many influences.

Italian cuisine can be characterized to be very simple, with many dishes that have only four to eight ingredients. Italian dishes are based especially on the quality of the ingredients, rather of the elaborate preparation. The ingredients and recipes vary a lot by each region. Many recipes that once were regional adapted through the centuries.

The "king" cheese and wine are a major important part of the Italian cuisine. As we can see in this cookbook, the food and culture are very important to the Italy. You can easily adapt your recipes by adding or removing ingredients, but you need to keep the important ones while doing this: the extra virgin olive oil, cheese, chili or parsley. Keep in mind that the quality of the ingredients it's the most important thing while trying to cook Italian recipes! I hope you found this cookbook interesting and very helpful, and that your cooking skills were improved while preparing our proposals.

Printed in Great Britain
by Amazon